Champion Speakers

Champion Speakers

Copyright © 2017

By: P Ryan Falkenberg

Devon, Alberta, Canada

www.RyanFalks.com

All rights reserved. No part of this book may be reproduced in any form by photocopying or by electronic or any other mechanical means, including information storage or retrieval systems, without permission in writing from the copyright owner of this book. The opinions and conclusions drawn in this book are solely of the author. The author bears no liability in connection with the use of the ideas presented.

1ST Edition

3

About the Author

RyanFalks.com was founded by Ryan Falkenberg to share my passion for public speaking with the world.

This book represents a desire to share everything I know about public speaking. My mission is to develop and instill confidence in our clients through the power of effective communication, and,ultimately, to achieve a lifetime full of happiness, significance and success.

I've struggled with communication from a very early age and was always fearful to speak my mind and share my thoughts and feeling with others. The lack of communication skills held me back from achieving my goals and, unfortunately, was the downfall of my first company.

It wasn't until I focused on overcoming my communication barriers that I eventually joined a public speaking program. I never thought I could develop into a public speaker. Speaking in front of a large group was an enormous fear for me. Speaking to my friends and family was already difficult enough, and most of the time, I would shy away from speaking to anyone. In the beginning, I didn't think this was something I could do. It was completely outside of what I thought was possible for me to accomplish.

Growing up with a shy attitude, being afraid to speak my mind, and always feeling nervous to talk in front of groups, I was fearful to take a chance on myself. My mentors pushed, encouraged and kept me involved in the program until I really started to be comfortable with it. If it was not for their support and the inspiration to step out of my comfort zone, I would not be the same person I am today. This program built my confidence up to an extremely high level, so much so that I'm now able to write this book.

Over my years of public speaking, I've developed many new skills, heightened my confidence and realize my own potential. Now, I have the opportunity to change other people's lives. I've hosted and chaired speaking events, spoken to numerous groups and met so many fantastic people. All of this would not have happened if I didn't take the chance to change my life and seize the opportunity staring me in the face.

The most rewarding part of public speaking is seeing the enormous change in my client's confidence. I have the ability to evaluate and make suggestions to my clients, but when they incorporate it into their own words and they see results, it's the most rewarding feeling. Seeing the new-found confidence gained when clients show a presentation makes it worth all the effort.

I'm not the most captivating or charismatic public speaker in the world. There are speakers out there who sound better than me, speak superior to me and clearly have better English skills than me. But what I do offer is: I'm completely authentic and personally work with each of my clients. My core values are the essential principles I live by, each and every day. They are to be honest with everyone I know, to help those who want my help and to always put in the most effort. When I give my word to help someone, I see it through to the end.

I know if I can make this change in my life, then you can to. I'm not any more dedicated, imaginative or inspired. The only difference between you and me, is when I had the opportunity to change my life, I took it. Taking a chance and investing in yourself, will always pay off.

My ultimate goal is to provide tools for my fellow speakers to get an audience to take action, to take a chance on themselves and to improve their lives. As a speaker, when you persuade more, it means that people are believing in what you're saying and they're being encouraged to believe in themselves more, today, than what they believed in yesterday. This results in people taking action and making changes in their lives, for their family, their relationships and their careers.

For me personally, public speaking has been the key ingredient in overcoming my life fears. Fears that were major hurdles in my life just started to disappear as I got more involved with speaking. What speaking does is build your confidence. It gave me the confidence that I never had before. And over time, I've not only become capable, but generally eager to handle any situation, to speak in front of any group and to help others build their confidence.

Today, there are few choices in life I will hesitate to make a decision on. I truly jump into the water, feet first, because I have the confidence that no matter what happens, I can handle the situation. Though it may not work out the way I initially thought it would, I believe in myself, and in the end, things will work out. When the right opportunity is presented to me, I take hold of it and jump right in.

Fundamentally, speaking has given me the confidence to believe in myself, to believe in the people that are around me and to believe in the people helping me. This book is the culmination my years of experience, which I bring directly to you, because I believe in you.

CONTENTS

Introduction   12

Chapter 1: A Champion's Attitude and Motivation   16

Chapter 2: Champion Speakers' Fundamentals   30

Chapter 3: Champions Connect   50

Chapter 4: Champions use Emotion   64

Chapter 5: A Champion Moves   78

Chapter 6: Champions Evaluate Everything   86

Chapter 7: Champions Make the Opportunity   94

INTRODUCTION

My father had a saying that still holds true today, "If you do something, do it right or don't do it at all." If all you put in is half the effort, all you'll get done is half a job. Half is never good enough, so I give it my all and put in my best effort every time. If you're not putting in your best, how can others around you do their best? Life is separated between who will put in the effort right now and who will wait until tomorrow. A champion leads by example, because they know others will follow.

My fear of speaking held me back, whether it was speaking to small group in a board room or just being with friends around the campfire. This anxiety over speaking, was the downfall of my first business. I was petrified to pick up the phone and talk with my clients: to get the sale, to do business, etc. It was from that failure, that I eventually learned that to succeed for my family, for my life and for my business, I needed to change. And that change was to become a champion speaker.

The end result of having the ability to speak and capture an audience is that the confidence gained here will apply to every other aspect of your life. Once you're confident about speaking, you'll have the same confidence to make quick and accurate decisions. Today, speaking is my number one asset. The passion I have for effective communication goes way beyond myself. I know that speaking is a learned skill and it can be taught to anyone.

I've been down that road myself. When my communication skills improved it had a direct correlation to all-around improvements in my life. Being a great communicator has been the reason for promotions, new opportunities and having the fortitude to start and run my businesses.

After you finish this book, some of you will take these ideas and really hone in on your presentation skills to create a fantastic product. Others will say, "That's pretty good stuff. I'm going to put it on the shelf and when I need it, I'm going to take it down to use it." Unfortunately, six months from now, that group will be in the exact some position they are today.

Everyone can be an effective communicator because if you communicate like a champion, you become a champion speaker. It's in you, if you want it.

Chapter 1:

A Champion's Attitude and Motivation

To be a great Champion you must believe you
are the best.

- Muhammad Ali

True champions have enough confidence to face any challenge and know, with certainty, they will be victorious. We hold these superstars in such high regard because they have reached goals that were once thought impossible. That ability to make the impossible possible is how life's greatest achievements are accomplished.

When we hear the word champion, what comes to mind? Our favorite athlete, the beloved Hollywood star or the adored singers rocking the main stage. Those are the easy ones to spot, and rightfully so. If you make it to that point, you deserve the accolades that come with that status. There are many types of champions, and you don't necessarily have to reach superstardom to become a champ. How about the single mom who works 2 jobs to provide for her family? What about the corporate negotiator who brings together 3 disparate parties to sign a contract? How about the speaker who pours out his heart and soul on stage.

Everyone has the ability to be a champion, and the fact is that greatness is in each and every one of us. The difference that separates greatness from mediocrity is our attitude towards success. Are you willing to put in the time, effort and dedication to do something truly special? Time is one of the most valuable resources anyone has. No one can make up more time It's always counting down, and that's why, for the champions, it's now or never. If you don't do it now, then when? Is it more important to begin that project, to practice your skills and refine your delivery or is watching videos a better way to spend your time.

The amount of effort you exert will drive your attitude towards either being great or just ordinary. The more effort used, the higher your confidence and belief in the successful outcome of your objective. Setting an example of the minimum amount work shows that you are not fully invested. The energy you put into yourself shows everyone how much you truly desire success. That amazing confluence of effort and energy becomes contagious. Those around you will get caught up in the buzz. When you put in a fully invested 100%, those around you will want to do the same.

Dedication, commitment and loyalty are motivation principles that lead you to success. What are you willing to sacrifice in order to ensure your goal is achieved? Will you get up at 5:30 to run for a half-hour before work? Are you committed to the cause and believe in it so much you are willing to do whatever it takes to achieve greatness? How do you treat your team members? Will you lead them to victory? Are you reliable and willing to be there when they need you?

Qualities of a Champion

The word *quit* is not in a champion's vocabulary. The champ pushes forward, even though they face bitter defeat. What this means is that a champion won't quit or abandon others. Instead he or she will do whatever it takes for the team's success. Winners win and they possess the will to do so.

Champions know that it's not about them. The greatest winners focus on the success of the big picture. They train and visualize every step it will take to be triumphant. They remember that no one is ever alone in victory. Who will help you on your journey? If you help the right people achieve their goals, you will achieve yours. This teamwork will create the right culture to help everyone develop unique strategies to deal with problems when they arise.

These champion leaders realize the skills they possess and will use them to bring out the best in people. The mark of influential top dogs is that they inspire others to surpass their own limitations and focus on the infinite possibilities that could exist. Rather than seeing faults in other people and using threats as motivation, they look for the good in people and encourage others to be better. They lead by example and use the positive situations in their lives to showcase how success can be achieved.

Champions don't back down when times are tough. Perseverance in situations that are uncomfortable, threatening, or even painful will define your character. What are you willing to stand up for? Whose back do you have covered? Commitment to the greater causes shows how willing champions are to travel through difficulties and navigate dangers just to see their visions become reality. The most important distinguishing asset is that they do it, not for their own gratification, but for the team's success.

The saying, "No pain, no gain," is a fixture in their hearts. And so should it be in yours. There is a point when you will have to make a choice to let the pain consume you, and give up, or to persevere ahead. Every team needs everyone to push through the pain to advance. When you're part of a group who has overcome obstacles, it unites everyone together to drive forward to achieve new goals.

A champion must leave his or her comfort zone and take risks. Those who are willing to take on different roles as situations require and to help others on their paths will have their efforts repaid in kind. If you are willing to relentlessly and continuously learn, you will grow more confident from every situation. What you give is what you receive, and the more you give the more you receive.

Taking a chance on something new is like jumping into a lake. Imagine, standing on the edge of the dock, looking down at the water and preparing yourself to jump in. You don't know how deep the water is, the temperature, or if there are any fish in there. You have a choice to make: in one hand, you can run back to shore and let the fear of the unknown devour your confidence; in the other, you reach out to my hand and we can jump in the water together.

Failure is Only a New Start

How you deal with failure is how you will succeed. It's true that people generally discuss their successes more than their failures, which makes it seem like success comes so easy. But let's get real: success is built on learning from failures and the desire to keep going, in spite of them. It's your choice to let a failure end your vision or let it simply be a bump in the road. I could have mailed it in and given up, but I chose to get up and face my fears straight on.

Analyze past failures to gain the wisdom for tomorrow. Learning from past mistakes is key to growth but more often than not, these painstaking efforts result in practically no change. People tend to classify failure only as something negative, and what's worse is that they just review and write a paper about what the failure was. End of story. But this should not the end of the story at all. Not all failure is bad. What's bad is not doing anything about it. Failure is a mindset regarding how you look at the situation. Was the failure inevitable, was it actually a good thing or was the situation completely out of control?

Who's at fault, who's responsible and who's to blame for this situation -- these are usually the sentiments that get passed around. The incorrect mindset is to see the problem as someone else's responsibility and to dodge any accountability for the situation. A culture of learning is much more productive, and people feel rewarded when they realize what can be learned from failure.

Failure can be a wide open spectrum from deliberate deviance to careful research. People who deliberately violate a situation must obviously be held responsible. However, those who are deliberate in their actions must have been motivated in some way. Likewise, failure from careful research may in fact result in praise, because the information generated in the research may be more valuable than if the situation would have succeeded.

Realize that not all failures are equal. A deep understating of the situation's context and causes will help you avoid the blame game. There are 3 fundamental failure types: avoidable, complex and intelligent. Avoidable failures are typically measured as bad. When an avoidable failure occurs, it's the result of improper training, lack of support or inappropriate attention of detail. Complex failures are due to the compounded or multipart combinations of problems in the situation. These complex failures offer new perspective and insight into how the situation is being handled. They can ultimately help find new processes to avoid future failures. Intelligent failures are usually the good failures that create a culture of growth. This could be test marketing a new product or service to clients. You may find out that what you thought would be the next billion dollar idea is actually not what your clients want.

Failure should be our teacher, not our undertaker. Failure is delay, not defeat. It is a temporary detour, not a dead end. Failure is something we can avoid only by saying nothing, doing nothing and being nothing.

- Denis Waitley

Create your own culture of learning from these mistakes. This will allow you to be comfortable to take a chance and be responsible for the outcome, positive or negative. Changing your mindset from "Who's to blame?" to "What happened?", will change the way you look at failure. Having the proper mindset will allow an unbiased look at your own situations. Make it your goal to detect possible problems before they become a disaster.

Universal Motivation

Everyone is motivated some way, and nothing is ever done without some kind of intention. Unfortunately, most people have no drive to tackle or complete anything. But if we look closer, there is always a motive behind this inaction. You might think the person who's watching 8 hours of TV every night is not motivated. But in fact they are. All of us are motivated differently, and what may be encouraging to you, might not be to another. Finding the true foundation of motivation behind actions or inactions will uncover real intentions, incentive and drive.

Have you ever overheard someone talk about that guy and say, "He's just not motivated." Most people believe that you're either motivated to go out there and realize their dreams or you're not. The motivated folks go out and find a great job, get huge contracts and make the big money, while the rest of the unmotivated group head to work, do their job and go home. This group, which may be considered unmotivated, is in fact motivated in their own way. Finding the motivation behind a successful individual can be easier to point out. Perhaps it's money, title, power, control, authority. The seemingly unmotivated person who only goes to work is motivated differently possibly by safety, security or keeping the status quo.

When I was younger, I was that guy on the couch watching TV for hours and hours a day. You may think I wasn't motivated, but in fact I was. I was motivated by the ease of doing nothing, the safety in just sitting there, and the comfort in not dealing with anything else. Many people don't want to deal with reality and would rather be consumed by a show, movie, etc. Later, when I realized that this can't be the only way to live, I discover so much more, like communicating with others, getting physical exercise and challenging myself to get out of that safety net.

To find people's, or your own, foundation of motivation, look deep into their actions and ask why. Why does this guy want to sit on the couch and watch TV? Why does this person want to be successful? When you finally determine the why, you're able to encourage yourself or those around you to take on new challenges, push yourself beyond what you're comfortable with and, above all, stimulate that spark inside of you to want to achieve more.

Regardless of what you do, people's actions are performed for their own reasons. Those who are responsible for their actions, will take responsibility for the consequences and will learn from the situation's outcome. Likewise, those who don't take responsibility for their actions will still act in their own self-interests, but will often learn nothing from the situation.

People only change when the alternative is worse. At some point in your life you have said the words, "I need to make a change." It might be for a job or for a relationship, but how often does the change actually happen? People will keep the status quo as long as they can, because the alternative, the change, is too tough. It's only when the situation becomes too tough that a change will happen. This change usually happens fast and when someone's back is against the wall. The thing to remember is that whatever path is the easiest people is the one people will most likely follow. If something is too tough, it won't happen. Just remember that successful people are able to navigate through the tough times and still make fast, accurate decision.

Pride can be the most powerful motivator. When you take control of your actions, that pride in your skills and knowledge will be the best reason to keep the momentum going. Those who have conviction, passion and belief in their insights and ideas, will begin to focus less on the money and more on message. When you focus more on the message, people will buy more into you.

Make the Change

Want to make a change in your life? Then deal with change now. Confront it, own it and adapt to it. Finding the silver lining in any situation can be a great way to see the change from a new perspective. Play devil's advocate with yourself and outline the pros and cons. What are some of the items that work out positively and what could have been done differently? Sometimes, finding the humor in the situation can lighten the mood enough get the conversation moving. Use tact with emotional situations and be aware of other's feelings. Some change just isn't funny.

Keep a positive perspective on the change. Being optimistic, constructive and helpful will advance the adoption of the change. However, being negative and projecting undesirable emotions will hinder the change. This mindset also includes a philosophy of "Don't stress out over being stressed out." Your thinking about stress actually has a negative physical reaction in your body. Funny enough, if you believe that you're stressed, you will become stressed. To overcome this, think about what the stress is accomplishing. Is the stress holding you back or is the stress simply about the unknown future? With the right mindset, stress can be a good thing. But only if you want to see it that way.

Highlight what your values are and focus in on them. The most important things to you, like family, relationships and personal pride, will bring stability to the change. Even listening to music or watching a movie can generate a cushion to fall back on that is consistent and won't create feelings of worry or trouble. Also, realize that there is nothing in this world that's truly certain and that you can't always expect stability. The world is constantly changing. There are always new products, new processes, etc. And we are always adapting to these constant changes.

The biggest way to accept change is to simply accept it. What has happened in the past is now the past. Fight for your future. Though some changes are out of our control, what we do about it and how we respond to it is free for us to decide.

Chapter 2:

Champion Speakers' Fundamentals

Words create emotional images in our minds, and each word impacts us differently. Champions focus on what they are trying to accomplish and eliminate those things that either complicate their presentation or aren't necessary. Any presentation should have a justification for each and every word, Illustration, testimonial, or slide. There must be a reason and rationale for why everything is said, shown or inferred.

Everyone wants success, but there are no guarantees. However, the chances of you being massively successful are greatly increased for those who become an effective communicator. If you polled the great leaders, like Steve Jobs, Elon Musk or Richard Branson, they would say the number one quality of a leader is to be an effective communicator.

Anyone that can't communicate properly is at a significant disadvantage. As a speaker, your goal is to inspire and create conditions to motivate those around you. If you're not a great communicator, it will be difficult to effectively relay information to your audience. The good news is that effective communication is a learned skill that can be taught. With determination and the desire to succeed, you can master public speaking as well.

Honesty is an important, fundamental psychological trigger. The audience can tell if stories are made up or embellished beyond a reasonable amount. You should never include white lies, smoke and mirrors or excessive exaggeration in your communication. Honesty is the essential key to authenticity

Champions understand the basic, fundamental process of how communication is relayed from one person to another. Basic skills, like using proper grammar, vocal variety and even memorizing a few lines here and there, will help you to influence your audience.

As humans we have the basic need to communicate with each other. We are extremely social and must hear, see, and even feel other people. Look at the phenomenal success that social media has had over the last few years. That's, just from the connection we make with each other. We're able to communicate with the masses practically anywhere in the world, at any time in the world, and we all can get that feeling of connection that brings the world together.

For many people public speaking is their #1 fear. Yet, each day we have no problems speaking to our friends, family and coworkers. To take it a step further, many people send audio and video messages to social media in an attempt to go viral and don't think anything of it. So, why do we feel different when we speak in front of a large group? Why do we get so much wrong information, mixed messages and even missing communication? To begin let's break down communication to its basic structure.

Communication is the imparting or interchange of thoughts, opinions, or information by speech, writing, or signs

- Dictionary.com

As humans we communicate via three basics methods:

1. Verbal (what we say)
2. Actions (what we do)
3. Optical (what we see)

Notice that methods 2 and 3 are both visual: we see what people do and we see what is written with our eyes. Did you know that verbal communication is also visual? When you speak, or are spoken to, our mind translates that information into mental pictures. The more vivid, emotional and descriptive the communication, the better the mental picture will be and the higher the chance the message will be received and recalled.

Why do we need effective communication skills? The reason is simply that when we send or receive a message, it needs to be sent, processed and understood by other parties. As a message is passed between people, it can be scrambled, twisted or misinterpreted.

Though many interactions are completed without actually talking to one another, like texting or sending a quick email, all the major items in your life will require face-to-face contact. When talking to a doctor, you would need to explain what's happening to you or a family member. If buying a house, you need to talk to a real-estate agent and a lawyer. Or take job interviews for instance; they're only complete once a potential employer has met and seen you. There is no "Buy Now" button for these situations.

Sending a Message

Communicating a message is a four step process. Bu remember, within each of the four steps there can be opportunity for different interpretations, misunderstanding, and an overall breakdown of the intended message.

1. Sender crafts the message.

The message must first be created, thought out, and visualized in the mind of the sender.

2. Sender communicates the message.

The sender then translates the visual picture in their mind into words, actions or illustrations.

3. Receiver collects the message.

The receiver then sees or listens to the words, actions or illustrations that are presented to them.

4. Receiver processes the message.

The receiver then processes the messages back into their minds as a visual representation of the message.

As you can see the need for clear, simple and descriptive messages is extremely important. A misfire on one of the steps, and your messages can be easily misinterpreted. The coming topics will show you exactly how to communicate effectively using simple and organized speeches to send effective messages to your audience. Remember the 3 Ss of communication: short, simple and specific

Structure

In order to communicate your message effectively you need to be clear, concise and most of all organized. The message must be conveyed in a systematic manner that will lead the audience on a journey. Every good message, communication or speech follows the same format, no matter if its 30 seconds or 45 minutes. There will always be an opening, a body and a conclusion. Take note that the speech is divided into 3 parts, as you will see the number 3 all over this organizational method. I've dubbed it the Power of 3.

The 3 parts of the speech (the opening, body and conclusion) can also be combined with the Power of 3 "Tell Them" philosophy. Tell them what you're going to say, say it to them, and then repeat what you have told them. We can then combine the "Tell Them philosophy with the 3 parts of the speech to get the ultimate speech outline: Opening (Tell them what you're going to say), Body (Tell them) and Conclusion (Tell them what you have told them). Let's now examine each part of the speech in detail.

Speech Opening

The opening of your speech needs to be energetic. The audience will know within the first few seconds if you are authentic, if you are confident, and if there is something in it for them. The champion's speech opening is divided into 5 parts: grab their attention, what's in it for them, the hook, the outline and a creatable statement.

Part 1

Grab their attention. Let the audience know you are talking and that they need to hear what you have to say. The first 5 seconds of your opening needs to be crafted in a way that the audience will be intrigued, feel confident that you are the expert, and become curious to know more. These are some techniques that you can use to open up the opening of your speech: use a daring statement, present a new spin on a tired cliché, state an ideal or moral, recite a quotation, tell a self-deprecating joke, pose a question. Example:

Hi, I'm Ryan Falkenberg and I change people's lives.

Part 2

What in it for them. The main reason why people will listen to your speech is because there's something in it for them. The audience will subconsciously ask themselves: what's in it for me, what are you offering, and why should I listen? There must be a statement about the final outcome the audience will reach from listening to you. Example:

I help people overcome their fear of public speaking to deliver amazing results.

Part 3

The hook. This is the specific reason for your talk and relates to the *how* from part 2 of the opening. This part will show how to get to the final out outcome that was just stated. It should involve an emotional reaction to gain freedom, to gain happiness, or to become more successful. Example:

I'm going to show you how to successfully captivate your audience from the moment you begin your presentation.

Part 4

The fourth part of the opening is to tell them what you're going to be talking about. These are the takeaways. They will work hand in hand with the body of the speech, discussed next. Here we state the three main points that support your topic. State the 3 main points in your speech body, this is where you tell them what you're going to be talking about. Example:

What we are going to be talking about is an easy way for you to gain confidence, remove fears, and do it less time.

Part 5

The creatable statement. The final segment of the opening is to make you the expert. The audience is looking for guidance and you will direct them to a certain outcome. There should be a sense of research that directly supports your topic. Example:

You probably already know that effective communication is critical to advance your career and business, but did you also know that research has shown, most adults will stop listening to your message within the first 1 minute unless there's something in it for them.

Speech Body

Organization of your speech is key in guiding the audience through your talk. The main points should follow a logical progression that supports the theme of the speech. Identify each point and focus in on the order that makes the most sense:

- Main Point 1
- Main Point 2
- Main Point 3

This is the place to "Tell them".

Each main point can then be broken down into sub-points. Remember to use stories to illustrate your points. In fact, a personal story is the best way to connect with the audience and make for a memorable experience. Every sub-points doesn't necessarily need to be included in your point, so choose the best options that work with the Main-Points:

- Sub-Point A - like the opening of a speech, grab the attention of the audience.
- Sub-Point B - explain the purpose of the main point in detail.

- Sub-Point C - how did the point make you feel
- Sub-Point D - how will it affect the audience
- Sub-Point E - end with a call to action.

Speech Conclusion

Restate or summarize the opening of your speech and explain how, referencing the main points in the body of the speech, all this information connects together. Avoid adding any new information

Finally, close with a call to action. Empower the audience. Inspire them to do something.

Additional items to keep in mind:

- End on the positive note
- Make an impact. Strive to be memorable

- Maintain the organization techniques throughout the speech

Conquering Fear

The oldest and strongest emotion of mankind
is fear, and the oldest and strongest kind of
fear is fear of the unknown.

- H.P. Lovecraft

You don't know what you don't know. I had it all figured out. I ran my own business and was doing well. People were handing me so much work I hired subcontractors. It was all fantastic, until the economy flipped and there wasn't a contract to be had. At this time, I didn't have any of the fundamentals that would allow me to ride out the economic disaster. Eventually, I had to close down my business. I was forced to build my way back from scratch, learning the right way to build a company, run a business and persuade and influence people.

When I lost my business, I was scared. Would I be able to support my family? What would I do for money? Would I get back on my feet? The unknown can be the scariest place to be, if there is no one around to support.

People naturally think negatively about themselves. They mistakenly believe that their feelings of inadequacy are shared with the group. Remember growing up in school and the teacher would always remind the class there's no such thing as a "stupid question". The reason there's no "stupid question" is because most of the time there's another student with the exact same question. The same theory applies to speeches. There will always be a certain number of people who believe in what you're saying. Have passion, be engaged and be authentic with the audience, and they will recognize those qualities in you.

Speakers just starting out sometimes feel their speech is boring. However, it's probably the presentation material that's boring, not about you as a person. Focus on the way in which you present yourself. Find your wow moment and exude confidence. Confidence will allow you to always have great topics to discuss.

Visualization is the key to overcoming anxiety. It's the technique of creating a mental image of future events. We close our eyes and see the possible outcome of a goal we want to achieve. People from all walks of life practice this, from sports figures to musicians to entrepreneurs.

I rehearsed making the same shots countless times in my mind.

- Jerry West (NBA hall of famer, aka Mr. Clutch)

Visualization

Visualization works because seeing is believing. Your brain's imagery is the same for the visualization perception as it is experiencing something for real. Practicing visualization techniques will prime the body and mind to be ready to deliver an outcome that's consistent with your mental image.

There are two types of visualization: Final and Process. Final visualization is where you imagine what the final outcome will look like and how it will make you feel. Process visualization is where you go through each step involved in the event, almost like a mental movie.

To practice process visualization for speeches, I suggest the following:

1. See yourself being introduced and walking on stage
2. Feel yourself standing in front of the audience. Looking around. Breathe.
3. Rehearse your speech, opening through conclusion
4. Think about how you will smile, Think about your tone. What's your look? How will you stand, hold your hands, or move around?
5. Speak your final words. Listen to the applause and walk off the stage with confidence

Relaxation means releasing all concern and tension and letting the natural order of life flow through one's being.

- Donald Curtis

Achieving relaxation

Achieving relaxation in stressful situations is possible with dedicated to maintaining a positive frame of mind. Your body and mind are connected more than you realize, and when you calm your mind, the body will naturally calm as well. The following techniques are universal for all stressful or anxious situations you may experience. They can be used individually or combined together for more effective stress reduction.

1. Breathing - Catch your breath and control it. Slow it down, breathe from your diaphragm, and expel all the air in your lungs.

2. Tight Muscles - Focus on the areas of tightness on the body. Breathe, tighten the specific muscle, and release the muscle to its natural state. Also, you can raise your arms shoulder height and rotate them in small circles

3. Count Backwards - Count slowly from 3, 2,1. Remember to breathe out between each count

4. Erase those Negative thoughts -

5. Think Positive Thoughts: I am confident. I know what I'm going to say. I feel cool, calm and, collected. I am going to do it

How do you practice, will you sacrifice time and effort now to gain the future you want tomorrow. I admire work ethic above almost anything else. I think it should be reinforced that practice makes perfect. You have to be diligent with what you want. Apply and motivate yourself to achieve your vision.

You have to do for yourself by yourself and then you can do for other people.

- Tupac Shakur

They say practice makes perfect, and speaking is no exception. When a presenter, for a keynote speech or any other public speaking engagement, gets on stage and really nails it, it's because of hours and hours of rehearsal. The best public speakers rehearse their speeches many, many times until it's perfected. There are many ways to practice, here a just a few:

2. At home in a quiet place
3. In front of a mirror
4. Video or audio record yourself
5. Rehearse with your mentor
6. Present to family or friends

One key ingredient that people tend to miss is to practice the exact same way you will deliver it. Hockey players practice every day throughout the season, and one message that keeps coming up is if you practice hard, you'll play hard in the game. Practice your talk exactly the same was you intend to deliver it. Stand as if you're on stage and speak at the same pace you expect. Speakers delivering a keynote speech will spend weeks practicing before presenting.

Never giving up can be the toughest challenge of all. It sounds so simple and easy: just keep going, just stay on track, just do it. However, when you're stuck in the middle, there are a few techniques and motivational tools that will keep you positive as you push forward.

1. Have a desire that borders on obsession about the success you crave. The greatest leaders in the world are on the verge of being completely obsessed with their idea. Their vision is of top priority, and they will do anything to guarantee it will happen.

2. Celebrate the little achievements. Take the time to pat yourself on your back and celebrate the goals achieved.

3. Look to someone who has persevered on and reached their goal.

4. Reach out to someone who can mentor you in the right direction.

CHAPTER 3:

CHAMPIONS CONNECT

Who are you trying to persuade? Who are you trying to sell to? Who are you trying to influence? When trying to connect with the audience, you need to know the answers to these questions. Many speakers don't even know who their target audience is. To really connect with the audience, you must target this group of people.

Demonstrate you're a person of integrity. In the course of dealing with people, sometimes you will realize that you're out there for a different purpose than you originally thought. When people open up to you, remember speak to them as a complete person. Keep it in mind that it doesn't always have to be about success, sometimes you need to be there just to help people.

Sometimes, it's more important to help people and solve their problems. Take the time to do it. Remember, in all your dealings, to act as a person of integrity. Take the values you hold important: Do you value your own life? Do you value the lives of those who are desperate? Do you put aside potential returns and recognize the need to help others.

First Impressions

You never get a second chance to make a first impression. Everyone knows this old cliché, and the reason why it won't disappear is because it's true. A first impression happens only once, and it's usually fast. Within a single moment of meeting someone, they will make a decision about you, whether they like you, trust you, feel comfortable with you, and once the judgement has been made, it's extremely difficult to change it. To put it simply, the better your first impression is the stronger your relationships and connections will be. People will tend to give more latitude and flexibility to those who make a great impression. Those who have a negative first impression will spend a lot of needless, wasted energy changing that perception into a positive one.

If you don't plan, you plan to fail.

- JT Foxx

Preparation is the best way to make certain your first impression is a positive one. Before a meeting, know who the key players and what the motivation is behind the introduction. Make a list of 3 questions or statements that can be used to break the ice and show you care about meeting them. These questions or statements should be crafted to showcase your knowledge and abilities, or demonstrate that you have done your homework. You can go one step further, video record yourself and review the playback to see how you come off. Taking the time to self-evaluate your strengths and areas in need of improvement will definitely pay off in the long run.

Be mindful of how you act, how you move and how you speak. If you are so apprehensive that your hands are shaking and voice is stuttering, the introduction could be considered negative just on the merits of being awkward. Attempt to control those feeling of anxiety by keeping movements very simple. Use the prepared statements to bring up topics. And most of all, think positively. If your mind thinks positive, you will show that confidence in the introduction. However, if your mind is negative, the first impression will also be just that Standing or sitting straight, paying attention, and having a firm, friendly handshake are key factors in a positive first impression.

Find some common ground you share with the other person. The shared element doesn't need to be something profound, think of smaller things like what city you grew up in, the schools you attended or the cool piece of new technology you both have. Part of doing your homework is doing research on the people you will be introduced to. Use LinkedIn, Facebook and other social media to gain some insight into the people you are meeting. Pay careful attention not to overstep though. Research can easily go way overboard and come across akin to stalking, which will completely ruin the first impression.

Your Homework

We talk a lot about preparation, doing your homework, being organized, and rehearsing. These are the key factors in developing and building confidence. Attempting a presentation when you're cold, unprepared and at a loss for words will increase your chances of a crash and burn disaster, which may further reduce your self-esteem and lower self-confidence. How much time are you willing to invest for success?

You don't climb mountains without a team, you don't climb mountains without being fit, you don't climb mountains without being prepared and you don't climb mountains without balancing the risks and rewards. And you never climb a mountain by accident - it has to be intentional

- Mark Udall

The best speakers in the world make it look like it comes easy or naturally, but the truth of the matter is that they spend countless hours honing, refining and improving their skills until they get it perfect. The ultimate goal is to have poise, composure, and calmness in the way you present yourself.

Deliver the message with impact to make your words memorable and your message significant.

Know your material. You must be knowledge about the message. Have you put in the time and effort it takes to completely understand the topic and be able to relay that information to the audience?

Did you check out the room prior to the event? Being comfortable in this environment will go a long way to build your confidence. Arrive at the location early, map out the room in your mind, even go up to the front, where you will be speaking, and visualize the delivery of your presentation. Is there enough light? Is the temperature okay? Are there any other distractions (outside noise, late audience arrivals, etc.)?

Planning and organizing these details lets you know where you need to be and how to get there. Have the date in your calendar. Know exactly how you will get to the event. Allot yourself enough time to get there and set up.

Rehearse - Practice makes perfect is so true, especially in public speaking. The more you speak, the more comfortable you are, and the easier it will be to find the words to express yourself.

I like rehearsals

- Matthew McConaughey

These are the best practices for a productive rehearsal:

1. Focus on remembering main points.
2. Run through the entire speech.
3. Avoid distractions, external noise, etc. (and don't hold any notes or paper that you don't plan on holding during the actual speech)
4. Visualize your presentation.
5. Ask for comments.

Topics

There's a million different things to discuss or talk about; however, getting too specific in the beginning may lose your audience or only hold the interest of a small portion of it. The most common topics to bring people in and grab their attention are:

- Success
- Mindset
- Health

Ask yourself, what's in it for your audience? Subconsciously, the audience will be asking the same question in their minds. What's in this for me? Champions share their experiences or understandings from their own perspective. Knowing the makeup and diversity of your audience will help you to craft a talk that is relatable, impactful and memorable. These are the audience variables to be aware of:

Age

Is the audience mostly under-18, Generation-Y, middle- aged or seniors. Explaining the relevance of Snapchat and Twitter with a group of seniors won't be as effective as if you were talking with a group of teenagers. Likewise, discussing the benefits of investing to the middle age group would have a much better response than when talking to seniors already in retirement.

Gender

What is the mix of male to female in the audience? The way you deliver the message to a primarily female group may be different than what's delivered to a majority male audience. Men tend to connect to actions, while women are more likely to connect to information.

Occupation

Are you talking with blue collar workers, white collar, entrepreneurs, or executives? Using technical language when speaking to a group of engineers will work, but using technical language in a group of fabricators from a shop floor will definitely lose their attention. Likewise, knowing something about the economic status of your audience will help to send the appropriate message. No matter who you're talking to, your message must be suitable for their knowledge level and how they run their daily lives.

Geographic Location

Where is the audience from? What is their predominant political orientation? What type of leisure activities are they most involved in. Up in Canada, you can discuss hockey all day long. But in the USA, hockey is not as popular, so best discuss baseball or football. Also, be sure you know the team everyone is cheering for. You can look like the hero when mentioning the major sports team; however, if you accidently mention their bitter rivals, the audience can be swayed to think you're not knowledgeable about them.

We talk a lot about preparation. Do your best to find specific info on the audience. Ask the host or other speakers prior to the start of the event. If you're still unsure, work the question into the speech opening. Asking questions to determine who you're talking to has two benefits. One, you can incorporate it into the opening of your speech and make it seem like it's routine. Two, asking question from the start will get the audience moving around, which will get their attention.

What is the audience looking for in your talk? What do they need to know? Poll the audience or the promoter about the knowledge level of the group. Have they heard your discussion before or is it brand new. If it's new information, you'll need to spend some extra time explaining the fundamentals. If the talk has been heard before, craft the speech to include new advanced information the audience wouldn't already have.

Identify the goal of your speech. Is it to simply pass on information, to entertain the audience or to persuade and inspire them to take action?

Who Cares What They Think About You

Care about what others think and you will
always be their prisoner

- Lao Tzu

We all feel the need to be liked and acknowledged; that's human nature. This can lead to spending too much time worrying about what other people think of you. Put this mentality behind you. When you are confident and know you're doing the right thing, you won't worry what others think.

Here are a few points to keep in mind:

It's your life. You are always responsible for you. People can tell you where to go, what to do, or what you say. But it's up to you to decide to do it. We are all judged by our actions. So, ask yourself: are you doing this action for yourself or for someone else?

You know what's best for you. People talk about what they think is best for you. But you should always consider is it actually the best thing for you or is it the best thing for them. Sometimes this statement comes up when someone wants you to take actions that they themselves don't want to do.

It's got to work for you. What works for 90% of people may not be a fit for you. We are all unique. And the truth is you must find your own way to get things to work.

Your vision is for your future. The vision you have is yours, and no one else's. You choose to walk along the path to success. Dreams don't come true - visions do.

It's only you, at the end of the road. Many people will always offer support, give their opinion, or judge what you're doing. But at the end of the day, you're the one who'll be standing there either successful or not.

Others will tell you what to do, but may never do it themselves. Everyone will give their opinion: "You should be in this..." or, "If a guy could..." These statements are always based on the dreams of those people making them.. Actions will always speak louder than word. Always ask this question: If that statement is true, then show me.

There's only so much time. Don't waste it. The most valuable commodity you have is your time. Don't waste it by worrying about what others think. Use all the time you have effectively. Put the effort into yourself, your projects and how you think.

Do these people really care? People talk smack all the time. Do you really believe that they have a true, deep interest in what you're doing? Remember, it's impossible to make everyone happy.

The fact is when you're speaking, the audience will probably have 20% all-in, loving you no matter what you say. Another 30% will like what you say, but want more proof, and 30% will be interested, but need to know you more. The final 20% are know-it-alls, who will be very difficult to connect with and influence.

Chapter 4:

Champions use Emotion

Make a connection to relate and appeal to the audience's emotional needs. The whole purpose of communication is to make a connection. As a public speaker, or even just chatting with colleagues, you want to connect with your audience on an emotional level. Champions will choose topics that relate to themselves and the audience. Relatability will help to cement this emotional connection.

Discovery consists of looking at the same thing as everyone else and thinking something completely different.

- Albert Szent-Gyorgyi

Discover Your Point of view

Personal stories about your experiences, where you came from, and what challenges you faced are the most effective way to relate the theme of your speech. When you are emotionally connected to your story, because it actually happened to you, it tends to have more conviction, persuasion, and influence. The audience will pick up on your passion and be drawn into it.

The following questions are about your life and what you do. These prompts can help remind you of stories you haven't thought about for years. This is the time to talk about yourself. It's an exercise to discover and develop your story.

Write a personal anecdote to accompany each one of the following questions. This will give you a library of personal reference material that you can dip into when crafting a speech or just making conversation with a friend.

Hobbies:

- What do you find relaxing? Exercise, music ,other interests?
- Why is this activity important to you?
- When you're engaged in the activity, how does it make you feel?
- What can others learn from your pastime?
- What value do you get from this hobby?

Sports:

- What sports teams do you follow and why?
- Have you played a sport, either recently or in your youth? Why?
- Did you watch a sports event that influenced you in some way? How?
- Were you the underdog and upset the other team? What made you feel this way?
- Who is your favorite athlete? Why?

Travel:

- What adventures have you been on?
- How did you get there?

- What influenced you to go in the first place?
- What did you learn?
- What made the journey worth the effort?

Education / Career

- What events led you to the here and now?
- What achievements have you been recognized for?
- Who are the influencers in your life?
- What goals have you completed? How did it make you feel?
- What goals do you have for the future? What's holding you back from completing them now?

Engage the audience with similar interests, by showing honesty and in sharing how they can make a change. Personal stories are the best way to add emotion. Anything that you're passionate about and that really happened to you will demonstrate authenticity and build a strong connection with the audience.

Your Message

Why is your message important? Why should people listen to you? What's the significance of your message? A good story is important, but that's only one aspect of relaying your message. As a speaker, you need to tell the audience what's in it for them. How can they can use the information you provide to make their lives better?

Open up and share your vision. Lead the audience in the journey. Some say that dreams don't come true, but visions become reality. When it comes to thinking about the future, the majority of people will usually have a positive, hopeful attitude. In the future, things will be better:I'll have the time to do this project or I'll be able to afford that product. The vision you have, once properly relayed to the audience, will inspire people to take action. Push the envelope and take on something new.

When dealing with people, remember you are
not dealing with creatures of logic, but with
creatures of emotion.

- Dale Carnegie

Know how your audience will react to you information and try to be at the same level as them. Testing information with others who are similar to your target audience is a fantastic way to experiment with information that people find useful. All major organizations have focus groups that test different material and give the feedback on what they think. Testing material should be an integral part of your workflow. Sometimes you may think your idea is the best idea ever, but your message completely misses the target. Having a support group to bounce these ideas off will pay dividends, and it will save countless hours of your precious time.

Creating a story that ignites passion, desire, and yearning to hear more comes down to crafting a message that follows the basic protagonist vs. antagonist format. Some ideas you can use to help your writing include:

- How you faced bitter defeat, but managed against all odds to come out winning.
- The time you took a chance and it ended up working out.
- When it was you against the world, and you were able to triumph over adversity.
- A conflict between you and someone important to you.
- An adventure that you went on that didn't go as planned, but you managed to deal with it.

- When you were the underdog and no one gave you a chance to succeed, but you did anyway.
- A heroic story of how you put your life on the line to save someone.

When your emotions break through and reach the audience, you will become more authentic and real to the listeners. Describing a scenario in too fine detail can be overlong, and you may lose the connection with the audience. A picture is worth a thousand words, so show them instead. Act out the scenario. If you're running in the story, run on the spot. If you're afraid in the story, show the fear in your face. When you have triumphed over adversity, show the confidence in your stance. Get into it. The more believable you are, the more the audience will buy in. Always remember no matter what it is you're selling, saying, or promoting, the audience needs to first buy into you. Once they buy you, believe you, trust you, then message will get through.

There is a point of adding in too much drama, so be wary of being overly dramatic or showy. Flopping around like a fish on stage for 15 minutes may seem like a great idea in your head, but could work against you and break any connection you have with the audience. This is another great reason to test your material with someone who can give you a proper evaluation and provide feedback.

The only way to change someone's mind is to connect with them from the heart.

- Rasheed Ogunlaru

Emotions are based on feelings. The story should tell how it made you feel, both before and after. Also, explain what put you into that situation, or what it felt like when your back was against the wall. Talking about your feelings in that moment will make you relatable. Most likely, people will either sympathize or know exactly what you went through.

Before you are a leader, success is all about growing yourself. When you become a leader, success is all about growing others.

- Jack Welch

If It's Personal, It's Important

When something affects your life or the lives of those you care about, it becomes important. Think about the parents of a newborn baby. They went from thinking about themselves to thinking about this new life that they are now responsible for. Once someone believes that something is important to them, they will then take action.

Your voice is the medium to express your thoughts, ideas, and visions for the future. But a voice also adds so many more elements, like curiosity, intrigue and interest. If your words relay the message, then your voice relays the emotion. For example, think of the different emotions conveyed by telling someone they gave "the best speech ever." It come across like the following:.

- { Sarcastic } the best speech ever
- { weird } the best speech ever
- { Passionate } the best speech ever

Words mean more than what is set down on paper. It takes the human voice to infuse them with deeper meaning

- Maya Angelou

The properties of your voice are volume, tone, and rate. Volume is how loud or quiet you are speaking. Various audiences will require different volume considerations. If you're in a boardroom with 7 people, your voice may be loud enough for everyone to hear. But it's not the same volume you'd use in a group of 97 people. That loud voice used with the larger group, if used in the boardroom, would have you yelling at the audience. Vocal volume should be always be moving up and down in time with your story. When sharing the backstory, your voice will be begin as soft and non-threatening. As you move the story closer to your main point, your voice volume should rise. Once on your main point, your voice should be loud and confident to emphasize, highlight and stress the importance of the words.

Tone is how deep or squeaky your voice is. The beauty of a voice is that everyone has a unique one. Your voice is your own, and it can be used to easily identify you. Think of how many times you say to yourself, I know that voice, or when someone comes on the radio or TV and immediately you know who it is before you see the image. Your voice can be part of what makes you unique and memorable. The vocal pitch must match the emotion portrayed. If you're talking about something enormous, gigantic or gargantuan use a deep voice for emotional emphasis. When discussing an item that is little, tiny or cute use the higher squeaky voice to portray the light and ease of the piece.

Rate is the speed at which you're talking. Are you fast and upbeat or slow and methodical? Diverse situations require a variety of different vocal rates. When trying to get through some seemingly boring material that must be said, but provides little value, up the vocal speed until you reach the main point, and then slow it down to illustrate the importance of the main point.

There are some definite qualities your voice needs. They are to be easily heard, to be expressive, to be fun and to be dynamic. Your voice should be easy on the ears and pleasant to listen to. It should express and match the emotions of the story. When you're having fun discussing your journey, the passion and fun will be reciprocated by the audience. Monotone voices will lose the audience within seconds. A dynamic voice that is always changing, moving, and active will engage and hold the audience's attention.

Use vivid descriptive words to paint a picture in the mind of your audience. The more vibrant the words are, the more interested the audience will be. This will allow you to create an experience. Below are some examples are of common words to replace:

- Use "fantastic" to replace "ok"
- Use "unforgettable" to replace "nice"
- Use "enormous" to replace "very large"

Clichés can be a great resource to relate to the audience.

*Cliché as a trite, stereotyped expression: a
sentence or phrase, usually expressing a
popular or common thought or idea that has
lost originality, ingenuity and impact by long
overuse.*

- Dictionary.com

Using incorrect grammar or word pronunciation can derail your speech and lose the audience. People will look for the faults, problems, or out of place words before identifying the positives of the speech. Practice any problem words that are difficult to pronounce and keep practicing until they become seamless and smooth. Using correct grammar and pronunciation will help the audience perceive you as trustworthy, educated and creatable.

Filler words can also detract and distract the audience, which may cause your message to be ignored. Using "Ah", "Um", and, "So", on a constant basis will have your listeners questioning your abilities and your confidence. These filler words convey a sense of being underprepared and not credible. Actually, any word can be a crutch. When I was first speaking, I used the word "Right" way too often. I would finish off my sentence with "Right?" looking for audience approval. If you're searching for the right word to say, avoid the filler words altogether and simply use a pause. The pause can be your greatest asset to show the audience you're in control and confident.

When sharing your message, consider each word special. If it doesn't add value to your speech, then remove it.

The Pause

Sometimes the words not said, the silence, can be the best motivator of them all. Mastering the art of the pause allows you punctuate the words. It will also help guide the audience from where one topic finishes and to where another one begins. The pause also works to control the rate and speed of the speech. When used correctly, the pause will emphasize the points in your discussion.

In other words, pauses "stick out like sore thumbs", and thus may occupy "beacon" positions in speech, serving to structure the entire utterance for both speakers and listeners. By subdividing speech into smaller segments, pauses probably contribute a great deal to the improvement of speech comprehension.

- Brigitte Zellner

Chapter 5:

A Champion Moves

It has been said that up to 80% of communication is nonverbal, meaning it's mostly visual. Your body speaks more than you know and can be used as a fantastic tool to add importance and clarity to your talks. The audience will evaluate what they hear, along with what they see, and pass judgement on your ability to connect with them. How you move, your expression, what you do with your hands will all communicate more emotions than just the vocalized words. Well thought out, planned and controlled movements will add substance to your speech. While shaking, nervousness and other indicators of anxiety will detract and compromise your connection to the audience.

There are four ways, and only four ways in which we have contact with the world. We are evaluated and classified by these four contacts: what we do, how we look, what we say and how we say it.

- Dale Carnegie

Own the Room

Own the room as soon as you enter. Your impact begins immediately upon your entrance. So, how should you enter the room? Here are the top 5 things you can do.

1. Preparation is key. Remember, knowledge is power. The more you know about who you will meet, the more likely you will be memorable, noticeable and able to capture everyone's attention.

2. Have a purpose. Why are you entering this room? What is the objective to this meeting? What goals would you like to achieve? When you have a goal there, is a clear direction for you to follow.

3. Dress for success. As stated above, 80% of communication is visual. The way you dress will say a great deal about you. Gauging the proper attire should be part of your preparation, because there are situations where you may be over- or under-dressed.

4. Be approachable. Wear a welcoming face and put away the phone. If you're trying to impress, don't be scrolling through the Facebook account and burying your head in the screen. Put the phone in your pocket and be friendly and open-minded.

5. Listen. The best way to show interest in someone is to pay attention and really listen to them. When you have actually heard what they are saying, you can comment directly on the discussion with an informed opinion.

The Hands

Hands can be used in a number of different ways. For example you can use them as a symbolic reference for other words, like using the peace sign or showing the number 4 using fingers. They can define a form or relate the size or the shape of an object. Also, they can relay emotions, from happiness with arms held up in excitement to furious anger with fists clenched tightly.

It's estimated that 95% of the reason why an audience will believe in you is because of a subconscious decision. The subconscious looks at your gestures as signals and clues about you. People will ask themselves if you are believable. Are you truthful? Are your authentic? The physical gestures you use are often more important than what you're saying.

Some people are naturals, but this can be learned with practice. And because gestures can be learned, you can be authentic and natural-looking too. People's decision whether they are going to buy into your idea or your product is subconscious. It's emotional. It's how they are reacting to their impression of you more so than what you have to say. What you say is usually from your right brain and what your gestures are doing stimulates the left-brain thinking.

The Eyes

The eyes are the gateway to the soul, so look people in the eye to make a connection. There are cultures around the world where making eye contact is forbidden, but not here. Don't shy away from making eye contact with anyone. Eye contact can make each individual in the audience feel like you are speaking to them personally. And when this connection is made, the audience will feel you are projecting authenticity, confidence and honesty.

Our eyes are well adapted to picking up on movement. If something moves out of the corner of our eyes, we tend move our heads to get a better look. This idea can be applied to your speech to better hold your audience. If your speech is monotone and you're standing still, the smallest distraction may grab the attention of your audience. Something as small as a cough in the blackguard can be enough to get noticed. The way to combat minor distractions is to always he the focus of attention. Move around the stage, add gestures, and show interesting visuals with fabulous content.

To make the ultimate connection, look at a person right in the eyes. Those around that person will know that I'm looking at that person, and the people around will be drawn in. As you talk and look directly at someone, everyone around recognizes the connection. Never just look in one direction or focus on just one side of the room. Walk across the room, then stop to look someone in the eye before moving on to someone else. When relaying something very important, stop, plant yourself, and look intently at someone. It's a very intimate connection, and it says "I'm speaking just to you." This helps create your charisma and authenticity in front of a smaller audience Step it up even further by directly approaching someone down in the audience.

Your expression is most often the main ingredient of the message. A speaker's face can communicate intentions clearly and visibly, leaving little room for doubt. Almost unknowingly, the audience will watch a speaker's face for signs that show passion, genuineness and their stance on the topic. The expression needs to match with what's being spoken. If you are discussing something sad, like the passing of a loved one, then your expression should probably not be a charming smile. A serious and respectful demeanour is much more appropriate.

The audience will be confused if your expression doesn't match your message.

Your Body Communicates

What to do with my hands has been a challenge of mine since I started public speaking. When I first started out, my hands stayed by my side, pointing straight down, and they stayed that way as if they were anchored to the floor. Later, I watched a video of my earlier speeches. My hands not moving an inch looked weird and distracting. I've learned that natural movements that match the rhythm of your words will make a connection with the audience without being distracting.

Stance and posture go a long way to demonstrate your confidence. If your shoulders are rolled forward and your posture is tilted down, the audience will have a sense of unease and this will detract from your abilities. However, being relaxed, standing up straight, and looking directly at the audience will show you're confident and prepared.

You should have a few go-to positions that look good and that you feel confident with. This is something that will need practice, usually in front of a mirror. The main positions you need to start with are the main position, the power stance, and the engaging position. Develop these for yourself, and you'll be consistent and never lost for how to stand.

When you're in front of the audience, move around the room naturally as if you're trying to bring people closer to you. Always avoid rocking or pacing, this is a sign of nervousness and can distract from the message. Move with purpose and find meaning behind your movements so that they keep time with your speech.

CHAPTER 6:

CHAMPIONS EVALUATE EVERYTHING

One of the most important parts of public speaking is evaluation. Champions use the tool of evaluation to be honestly critical of one's self. Understating what you did well and what areas needs improvement is the most powerful self-improvement tool available.

*Courage doesn't happen when you have all
the answers. It happens when you are ready
to face the question you have been avoiding
your whole life.*

- Shannon L. Alder

Likewise, evaluating others' speaking abilities is equally important. The more effective your evaluation, the more the speaker will benefit and improve. As an evaluator, you will learn to enhance your own listening and attention skills, while also focusing on the message from the speaker.

*To profit from good advice requires more
wisdom than to give it.*

- Wilson Mizner

Evaluation offers 3 benefits:

- To provide advice and praise
- To suggest areas that need improvement
- To build a speaker's confidence

It is important to remember that when you get any recommendation from someone else, you need to self-analyze the feedback, internalize it, and decide for yourself what to do with going forward. Some comments are easy to implement, such as removing "Ah" or "Uhm" from your vocabulary, while other comments will be based on a person's opinions or judgements. An evaluation is from one person's point a view. It's your choice to act on the advice or simply ignore it.

Top 10 Evaluator Do

1. Determine the objectives of the speech. What is the purpose of the speech? What is supposed to be accomplished? What are the speaker's performance expectations are and what are the goals of the speech?.

2. Give your undivided attention. Pay attention to the speaker's words, listen intently for proper vocabulary use along, keep an ear out for unique words and turns of phrase. Watch the speaker to see how they move, where they look, and when they add gestures.

3. Positive reinforcement. Make it a point to recognize each and every performance, not just the great or poor ones. Focus on what the speakers did well, how much they have improved, and if they achieved the objectives of their speeches.

4. Use the sandwich method for feedback. This is the gold standard for any type of feedback: Begin with something the speaker did well. Add a suggestion for something the speaker could improve. Wrap up with another item that the speaker did well

5. Give specific examples. Provide detailed descriptions of what was done well, along with what needs improvement. Feedback that is vague or too general can result in misunderstandings, and as a result, the comment could be overlooked and disregarded.

6. Be real, sincere and honest. Honestly is the best policy. There's no point in leaving out a suggestion that should be addressed. The speaker would rather hear about something that needs to be fix, than to not know about the elephant in the room.

7. Comment on how the speech made you feel. Emotion plays a huge part in connection with the audience. How did the speaker emotionally affect the audience? Was there laughter? Surprise? Anticipation?

8. Communicate your thoughts on the speech. The speech evaluation is your opinion, so use phrases like, "I think this was

done well," or, "in my opinion, this might work better next time," to connect with the speaker.

9. Document the evaluation. Use an evaluation form or write down some notes on paper about the speech.

10. Always end on a positive note. A large part of an effective evaluation is positive thinking. By the end of an evaluation, the evaluator should instill confidence in the speaker's abilities, motivate the speaker to continue to their next speech, and recognize the performance. Ending on a positive note sends that good feeling of positive energy all around the room.

Top 10 Evaluator Do Not

Don't count the days, Make the days count.

- Muhammad Ali

1. Avoid saying, "You should have ..." And also avoid sayings that are too direct and point the finger, "You should have," or, "You failed in your attempt."

2. Don't comment on the person. Evaluations are to be made on the speech itself, for example the organization, the information and the performance. There's no need to comment on the speaker's lifestyle choices or political and religious views.

3. Don't criticize too harshly.. Know who you're evaluating, whether they are a seasoned professional or just starting out, as the type of feedback can vary greatly. For a seasoned professional, commenting on small details to improve as opposed to everything they did well would be acceptable. This feedback would not work for a speaker just starting out. To help build confidence, this evaluation should focus on a few general items to improve and what was done well.

4. Don't give solely negative feedback. Hearing only about what was done wrong with the speech will damage the confidence of the speaker and could turn them away from speaking completely. Use the sandwich method of providing feedback.

5. Don't generalize. Always have specific details of the speech to comment on.

6. Don't be disingenuous. Only providing praise in the evaluation may be very gratifying for the speaker initially, but over time it will not help the speaker improve his or her skills. Covering up flaws can hurt the speakers immensely, if they don't even realize there's something that could be improved.

7. Avoid saying, "We think ..." Also avoid saying thing that are not based on your own point of view (things like, "Everyone is saying," or, "People think").

8. Avoid a critical face. As an evaluator a friendly simile can go a long way to can calm the speaker's nerves, set the tone, and ease any tension. An overly critical stare or expression of disgust can completely derail the speaker's train of thought. Keep in mind that as the evaluator, you will be looked upon for support and reassurance from others in the group.

9. Don't ruin self-esteem. Confidence, motivation and self-esteem can take a very long time to build, but with the

wrong word choice or tone,they can be destroyed in seconds. Be mindful and respectful of the time and effort that was given by the speaker to craft the speech.

10. Never end on a negative note. Ending on a negative note is like adding a "but" to the end of a statement. Think about it, "I congratulate you on your effort but ..." This sends the a negative message. Try ending with, "I look forward to your next speech," This fosters a positive and confidence-building wrap up.

Chapter 7:

Champions Make the Opportunity

Stress is an out of control epidemic in our society. It's a widespread problem that eats away at our lives, suffocates ambition, and distorts reality. No one in the world is immune from this rampant issue. We all deal with stresses, from work pressures to living healthy to family commitments. Anything and everything can be a stress. In the fast-paced lifestyles we live today, the majority of us have feelings of anxiety, apprehension and fear. To address this, we must find a better way, a new positive approach, a new way of thinking.

Positive Mindset

Many of our problems begin because we don't believe in the power of positivity. People who don't deal with well with stress tend to keep it hidden and disguised. Addressing stress boils down into two fundamental approaches, positivity or negativity (or rather, choosing to deal with stress or choosing not to deal with stress).

Stress is all in your mind but it manifests in different ways, physically. Stress truly is mind over matter.

- Kelly McGonical

Psychologist Kelly McGonical has analyzed stress for years. She asserts that when you're stressed and either can't or won't deal with a situation, your body goes through a physical reaction that makes you feel sick, lethargic and depressed. This tension can even constrict blood vessels and lead to heart disease or even worse medical conditions. This fact blew my mind! People who believe that stress is affecting their health have a 45% greater chance of dying. So, just to reiterate: if you think you're going to be sick from stress, boom, chances are you will be sick from stress.

Luckily for us, mind over matter works both ways. You can choose to think about the stress negatively (that you're going to die from it), or you can choose to think about it positively and thrive in the midst of it. Let me say this again, just so we all understand (and maybe grab a pen and write this down): you can choose to think positively about stress.

Again, looking at Mcgonical's research, when people truly believe in the positive mind, it has some extremely powerful results. What happens in the body when you're positive about stress? Your heart rate goes up. You can even feel this in your chest (it's actually the same as a good workout). The positive mind also allows your body to feel relaxed, even though stress is still there. The heart is pumping, and you can feel it, but your blood vessels are relaxed and open. This state can even help prevent heart disease.

There are 3 key approaches when dealing with the stress of speaking in front of an audience:

1. Practice. Practice. Practice. The honest truth is that practice makes perfect, and if you know your material inside out, you will be positive, confident, and relaxed.

2. Stress is all in your head. Remember, you are what you believe.

3. Think positive, act positive, and be positive.

Decisions made today can change your life. Decision-making skills change over time. Here are the 3 decision phases you will encounter in life..

- Decision phase 1 - when you're young.
- Decision Phase 2 - when you're a teen.
- Decision Phase 3 - when you're an adult .

Decision phase 1:

You see what you want, but you have no idea about the consequences.

Kids are always thinking with their mouth. To be honest, they will put anything in their mouth. When my daughter was 4, I looked over and she was chewing on a phone case, and then I caught my other daughter dropping a sucker on the floor. She looked at it, picked it up, brushed it off , and then stuck it back in her mouth. Children will eat or chew just about anything.

When a child is looking for food, he or she will focus only on it. For example, my daughter was in the kitchen and could see a box of cookies on the kitchen table. Now she was too short and couldn't reach the cookies, so she tried to pull the tablecloth and it's started moving towards her. So she pulled more, as stuff started dropping off the table, first a napkin, then a plate, until it looked like a garbage dump under the table. But she continued to pull more until the cookies wee just on the edge of the table, teetering, then they fell, and the box opened. She was covered in crumbs, cookies were scattered across the floor. She was crying, and frustrated that all the cookies were wasted. What a disaster! She knew what she wanted, but had no idea about the consequences of her actions.

Decision phase 2:

You know about consequences, but you totally disregard them.

Teenagers tend to think with only half a brain, and it's usually the right, emotional side. You will never hear a teenage boy say, "Hey guys, I'm not too sure about this." Teenage boys are ready to jump with both feet. For proof that teenagers totally disregard consequences, look no further than Johnny Knoxville and the Jackass TV series. These guys perform insane stunts that lack any sense of safety, but it was one of the most-watched TV series of all time.

Decision phase 3:

You know your wants and the consequences of those decisions.

What separates the champions from the rest is that they make quick decisions and are able to deal with the outcomes, no matter what. For the rest of us, we spend way too much time overthinking each and every little decision..

Our decision making skills do evolve and change with age. From kids having no idea about consequences to teenagers disregarding them to adults who know what they want, recognize possible consequences, and are still able to make fast decisions.

Nobody successful has made it on their own. Look at mega-stars like Arnold Schwarzenegger, in his prime he had a bodybuilding coach, an acting coach, a speech coach and a real-estate coach. All these coaches helping him, mentoring him and guiding him towards the realization of his vision. If this is good enough for Arnold, then it is good enough for me.

Be a Leader

Now more than ever, the world needs our next generation to be solid, experienced leaders who can effectively influence the future. Leadership and communication skills are not inherited. You're not born with those skills. They are learned. And the beauty is that everyone can learn to be an effective communicator. Everyone can learn to be an effective leader. Confronting new challenges and taking on new opportunities will always be worth the effort. Your understanding, knowledge and self-confidence will grow to fantastic new heights when learning from both failures and successes.

Like everything we do in life, effective leaders and communicators will be judged on their actions. How about you: did you achieve your goals, have you inspired others and helped them to achieve success? Some traits of a great leader are clear direction and vision for how to achieve a goal. Leaders will build a team that works together to achieve a common objective. Finally, a leader is the engine that keeps the parts moving to motivate, support, and recognize team achievements.

A coach and mentor provides the base fundamentals, along with the action plan, to achieve success. They keep track of what you're supposed to be doing, provide the background on why you're doing it and how you will get there, all while managing the expectations.

The coach is responsible for providing encouragement to keep teams focused on what they want to achieve and keep them motivated through the ups and downs. Coaches get up everyday knowing that success is within reach and you want it. They provide feedback on what's being done well and what could use improvement. This perspective is so important, because it allows others to use the experience from the coach without having to go through the same ordeals. Finally, a coach will set the standard of excellence for everyone to achieve. This includes goals that may seem extreme at first, but are achievable. Goal setting like this ensures everyone grows, steps out of comfort zones, and progresses as far as they can.

Your Life

Everything you buy must have value. The programs available are all value-based, so remember that the time and energy you spend will be worth it to achieve success. Dreams hardly come true, but visions become reality.

Stop talking about it and just get it done.

If you don't do it today, if you don't take the opportunity right in front of you, it won't ever happen.

Today is the day to change your life!

Manufactured by Amazon.ca
Bolton, ON